Goodbye, My Love

Goodbye, My Love

Christine Calhoun

◊ ◊ ◊

Appleton, Wisconsin

For Paul.

Chris & Paul's wedding, May 23, 1992

Preface

In April 2018, when I noticed how bad my husband's memory had become, I asked family members for their opinions. They said they had noticed changes for a while. This helped confirm my worries, so I prodded him to see his primary doctor. Although he was reluctant to go to the doctor, he finally acquiesced. The diagnosis was Mild Cognitive Impairment.

His physician referred my husband to an Advanced Practice Nurse Practitioner at a neurology practice. She gave him a battery of cognitive tests—draw a clock, count backward from 100 by three, name as many words that begin with "f" as possible, remember five words and repeat them when asked—all of which he had difficulty, especially remembering the words.

In August 2020, we returned to see APNP. The tests were repeated. I heard him struggle to answer the questions. His executive functioning was severely diminished from two years ago. At that time, he was diagnosed with Alzheimer's Disease mixed with vascular dementia. The Nurse Practitioner asked me to tell him of the diagnosis. She felt he had a right to know. Also, she advised it would be prudent if he stopped driving because of liability issues and scheduled a driving evaluation. Thank goodness, he voluntarily gave up driving. In October, he failed the evaluation. His driver's license was revoked.

On a beautiful August evening while we were sitting outside the family cottage, I told him the devastating news. I tried not to cry. He showed little emotion. His mother had died of Alzheimer's, so I thought he would understand the import of the diagnosis. However, I was unsure if he understood the gravity of the situation. I never again told him he had Alzheimer's.

In November 2020, I started to journal my observations/thoughts of our journey. On December 19, 2023, my husband passed away. This book is a chronicle of our journey.

November 20, 2020

When coming out of the grocery store, you were not behind me. Looking back, I saw you in front of the candy. You did not have your wallet. As you were walking back to the car, I saw a bulge in the pocket of your sweatshirt. You sat and took out a bag of candy. I asked you to take back the candy. Fortunately, no one saw you take the candy. However, you did not seem to understand it is wrong to shoplift.

You are constantly misplacing things and not remembering where they are. People's names are getting harder for you to remember.

November 24, 2020

You are putting soiled toilet paper in the waste basket. I put up a sign, "Please put the toilet paper in the toilet" by all the toilets. A cancerous lesion was taken off your head today.

December 3, 2020

A friend took you shopping for my Christmas stocking. You kept referring to her as a "he." I told you she lived with my sister, and you see them all the time. I fear you are slipping faster.

You again put soiled toilet paper in the basket. Again, I reminded you of the sign.

December 15, 2020

Yesterday, I found a used Depends and soiled toilet paper on the ironing board in the laundry room. The stitches in your head came off today. It healed well.

December 18, 2020

As I put clean underwear in the dresser drawer, I found wadded up soiled toilet paper in it. You were shocked it was there. Things are not getting better.

December 26, 2020

You were going to clean the hardwood floors. I noticed one of the containers was Round-up, the same color as the container of the floor cleaner, Bona. You brushed it aside saying you just picked up the wrong one. I hid the Round-up in the closet on top of the sump pump behind a pillow until I could give it to someone else. This was a profoundly serious lapse in your judgment, a big warning sign.

December 29, 2020

Toilet issues continue. There was a piece of soiled toilet paper on your side of the bed this morning.

For several years you volunteered for AARP's free income tax preparation service. Last year, you could not pass the qualifying test to be a preparer. This year you want to take the test to be a greeter, For the greeter test, I told you there is only one answer for each question. I am not sure you are able to pass the test.

You worked in finance your whole life, and last year, I discovered you did not know how to reconcile the checkbook anymore. I knew something was very wrong. Another red flag.

January 1, 2021

We had a nice New Year's Eve; we even danced a little. We played Yahtzee and Kings Around, and I decided we needed to play games every day. You had trouble playing both games.

January 10, 2021

According to the coordinator of AARP's tax program, you will not be a greeter because you no longer understand the procedures. You used to give blood monthly, and last year when you wanted to donate blood, you could not answer the questionnaire, so they rejected you. You were devastated. This morning, I found soiled toilet paper in your boots. How do I solve this problem?

You cried. I know you know something awful is happening to you. It is devastating to see this happening to the person you love. I feel horrible and helpless because there is nothing I can do.

January 19, 2021

Sex—I miss it. April 2020 was the last time we had sex before I broke my arm on May 19th. You were taking Viagra at the time but had to go off it because of other meds you were taking for your bladder. When we were younger, we could not keep our hands off each other. You were a great lover, always concerned with my pleasure. I am sure we will not ever have sex again. So many losses with this disease.

January 26, 2021

You did not recognize your niece on the Zoom call. You shoplifted again today. This time it was a candy bar at Aldi. I asked you to put it back. You continue to misplace things and then cannot find them.

January 27, 2021

You are starting to have problems dressing yourself. I typed up our contact information to put in your wallet because you could not tell me our street address and phone number.

February 6, 2021

Yesterday, we watched Rick Steves' program on PBS. It was about a Mediterranean cruise. You asked me if I would like to do that, and I told you I would very much like to do that. You seemed perfectly normal.

However, the next day you were quite different. You forgot you walked Jack an hour before. You usually thanked me for breakfast. You did not. Swearing all day, very frustrated, you could not find what you wanted. Throwing shoes. Clearly confused. Slamming drawers. Losing your glasses. You could not figure out how to put the cleaning pad on the Swiffer. I called a friend whose husband has Alzheimer's. It was wonderful to talk to someone who knows what it is like to be a caregiver. I knew it was the disease that was causing this behavior.

February 7, 2021

I found a pile of Depends underneath the bed in the guest bedroom, some clean and some dirty. I raised my voice. I apologized and told you I loved you very much. You said you knew.

February 15, 2021

I attempt to offer suggestions to help make things easier for you. Since you are constantly misplacing your glasses after walking Jack, I suggest you just leave them on the counter in the kitchen when you come back, but then you forget they are there. I type up a weekly calendar, but you ignore it. Are you having trouble reading?

February 17, 2021

A success for you today. You voted in the primary election. Before the election, I downloaded a sample ballot and showed you how to fill it out. Today, you remembered our address. I must remember to celebrate the successes.

February 24, 2021

We had our second COVID shot on Monday. Fortunately, neither of us had a reaction, other than a little soreness at the injection site. The Building Better Caregivers course offered through the Aging and Disability Resource Center was helpful. I found making goals a little difficult. Something always seems to get in the way of achieving it.

Another Depends under the bed. Your communication skills continue to deteriorate. You have trouble telling me what you want to say. You say the "thing" when you can't find the word you want. Rather than you tossing out used empty food bags, I am finding empty storage bags in the fridge.

February 25, 2021

You threw a dirty Depends at me this morning. I was horrified. You had never thrown anything at me before.

February 26, 2021

You attempt to read, but I am unsure if you can understand the words. I fear the disease is progressing rapidly.

March 2, 2021

You don't understand the concept of time anymore. While you sat at the dining room table, I asked, "What you are waiting for?" You replied, "Dinner." The time was 1:42 in the afternoon. I told you we don't eat until 6 PM. You must have been so bored. What was going on in your head? I felt helpless.

March 4, 2021

A good thing. Adult Daycare will reopen at the end of March. You seem okay with going.

March 7, 2021

Before going to bed, you did not know how to turn the light off over the sink.

March 11, 2021

You ate a lemon today. Did you confuse it with an orange?

March 16, 2021

I think the increased dosage of the antidepressant is helping. You are less angry when you are frustrated and seem on a more even keel. One good thing for me throughout this ordeal is I have learned to do things I would have depended on you to do.

We have an appointment with the coordinator of the adult daycare program. She will assess what daycare program is most appropriate for you.

March 20, 2021

You put your clothes on inside out and backwards. You can still tie your shoes.

March 31, 2021

Two successes. You figured out how to hang a refinished cabinet door in the kitchen, and we put together a raised bed for the garden. The toilet issues continue. I guess they always will. Shoplifting incidents have not continued.

April 7, 2021

The adult daycare gave us inventories to fill out—your food dislikes, favorite season of the year, favorite subject at school, just routine questions. You tried to fill them out yourself but couldn't, so I helped you. You started crying, saying, "I am no good anymore." I am heartbroken. I pointed out how successful we were in our recent projects. You said you were not sure you wanted to go to adult daycare. I said you would meet other people. You always enjoyed being around people.

April 8, 2021

I am relieved you liked adult daycare. You said people danced, and you told the others how you and I used to ballroom dance. There were also mentally stimulating games.

April 20, 2021

Incontinence continues. Wetting the bed last night. I remember the first time you wet the bed. You fell to your knees and cried and cried because you were so embarrassed. You had an accident at adult daycare. They requested I bring an extra pair of jeans and Depends. I am glad they wash your clothes after you have an accident. I hope there is a reason for this and that it is not due to dementia. I ordered a waterproof mattress pad.

April 21, 2021

The urologist increased the dosage of Flomax. He talked to me only, ignoring you. From observing your body language, I think you were annoyed with him. I was, also.

May 15, 2021

At the cottage, you wet the bed down to the mattress. I took the bedding to the laundromat. I bought a waterproof mattress for that bed, too.

May 18, 2021

I made an appointment with another urologist.

June 10, 2021

PSA was normal. You put your shorts on inside out and had difficulty tying your shoes, getting the laces into knots. You still do not remember going to adult daycare twice a week. At the YMCA, you wandered around and couldn't remember how to lift weights properly. Imagine that! You who was a workout fiend. I was afraid you might hurt yourself. You still seemed to enjoy being with the guys who were working out. In two weeks, your son, Eric, will be coming from California.

June 20, 2021

Reflecting on last week at the cottage. Other family members were there. You were different, afraid to swim or lie on your raft. I observed you standing at the front door looking down at the lake. You said, "No one is going to make me get into that fucking cold water."

When we were back home, you got lost for four hours while you were walking Jack. The police put out a Silver Alert on you and posted it on Facebook. There were 212 shares. The police finally found you about a couple of miles from our house. It was raining. Jack was cold, wet, and hungry; you were dripping wet but did not realize you were lost. I was exhausted. No more walking Jack alone. The next day you told the folks at adult daycare about the nice police lady you met.

July 2, 2021

I came home from an appointment to see you with Jack on the leash. You said you just walked around the house. I certainly hope you only walked around in the yard. On Monday, you left the stove burners on. I toured my first memory care facility.

July 26, 2021

I visited some memory care facilities. My oldest sister generously offered to pay for another day at adult daycare. The VA pays for two days a week. You are now there Monday through Friday, 8 AM to 3 PM. Adult daycare has been a lifesaver. You are in a safe place, getting the care you deserve and need, and I can go about my day. Caregiving is so exceedingly difficult.

The first week in July, I washed the bedding every day. Now I put a towel under the bottom sheet, two Chucks (bed pads) on top of the bottom sheet, and two towels over you. How do I feel? Often, I am jealous of my family who can enjoy summer while I am stuck. I am ashamed to say sometimes I resent you. I continue to go to a caregiver's support group twice a month. It helps to talk to those who understand.

August 9, 2021

You confused a lemon with an orange again. You asked what potatoes are. Your glasses were missing as well as the water bottle by your bed.

I took you to exercise class today, and you did okay with the instructor's instructions. You gained more than ten pounds. Eating everything in sight. I caught you before you ate raw shrimp.

August 12, 2021

You pulled out of your pocket a handful of Tylenol. I hid the bottle. I need to be patient and not get angry when you deny doing something. Alzheimer's makes the person who has the disease a liar.

September 3, 2021

You took three showers this afternoon.

September 9, 2021

I went to a meeting for an hour in the evening, and while I was gone, you urinated on the couch. No Depends on. It is increasingly difficult to leave you alone while you are not in adult daycare.

September 13, 2021

I washed all the bedding again today.

September 14, 2021

You wet the couch again. You did not remember doing it. Incontinence is a *real* problem. Earlier this afternoon in a lucid moment, you asked, "What is happening to me?" I am so sad and frustrated.

September 21, 2021

You are starting not to remember when you last ate. Today, you ate two bowls of soup and 45 minutes later you were eating two pieces of toast. Don't you recognize when you are full?

September 29-30, 2021

I had lunch with a friend. When I pulled into the garage, you came out of the house. Your lips were terribly swollen. You had a blank look on your face. I spoke to a nurse at your doctor's office and was told to take you immediately to the ER. She thought you had angioedema that can be life-threatening caused by an insect sting. It causes the lips to swell and can also cause the throat to swell, impeding breathing. As a precaution, you stayed in the hospital overnight. While in the hospital, you were extremely confused. You kept peeing and peeing through your hospital gown. The nurses didn't understand why. You were not embarrassed to take off your wet gown and stand naked.

Good news on the VA front: two separate exams will be scheduled. One for disability pension and one for Aid and Attendance. Aid and Attendance is income-based and helps pay for home health care or care in a facility. To qualify for a disability pension, the veteran's health issue must be service-related.

You stole a candy bar at Aldi today. I found it in your pocket when we got home. I thought shoplifting was over.

October 24, 2021

Your son was here for a long weekend, and you did not recognize him. You keep saying he was a "nice guy." We went for a hike with our niece and her husband and the dogs in a state park and had pizza for lunch. You went through your son's clothing in his backpack. At the airport, you hugged him and said you will miss him. When he was back home, your son messaged me and said deep down, he thought you knew who he was. He was the "Apple of Your Eye."

I am locking up your meds now.

November 4, 2021

You had what the adult daycare staff thought was a seizure. They were unsure if you lost consciousness. You almost slid off a chair, recovered quickly, and seemed back to your normal self. An EEG has been scheduled for November 23. Right before the test, I need to keep you in a sleep-deprived state for four to five hours, which I anticipate will be a tough job.

November 23, 2021

You did well during the test. Unexpected because you had to lie on your back and be still for an hour.

November 25, 2021

Thanksgiving

Dinner at my sister's and her partner's. It went okay. You fell asleep in a chair while others were talking.

November 26, 2021

We had leftovers at my sister's and partner's house. After dinner, you were eager to go home. That wouldn't have happened with the "old" you. You were a talker. Our niece who lives in Washington state is coming for Christmas.

December 1, 2021

EEG was normal.

You take your coat out of the closet. I tell you we are not going anywhere and ask you to put the coat back in the closet. You take it out and put it back on. Again, I ask you to put it back. We do this over and over.

December 7, 2021

You cried again, telling me how much you loved me. I know you do. I caught you picking a turd out of the toilet. You put your shoes on the wrong feet and tried to put your shirt onto your legs. Heartbreaking to see the changes in you.

December 27, 2021

Lovely Christmas at our house, although you didn't know what Christmas means. You didn't know how to deal with your presents and your Christmas stocking. We played Christmas charades. I have the after-Christmas blues, or is it the stress of caregiving?

I need to be more careful when I speak to you. You talk to yourself frequently, in an angry manner. How long will you know me? How long will I be able to care for you at home? I worry about money. I have been slowly losing you for years, and it continues unabated. One of the hardest things for me is to accept that the man I married is gone forever.

Your Veterans Service Officer said your honorable discharge from the Navy was due to migraines. He is going to look further into this. You never mentioned having migraines.

January 10, 2022

When I was helping you shower, you pooped. I never thought I would have to clean you up after you go to the bathroom. Alzheimer's robs the person of his or her dignity.

The cognitive exam is scheduled for a week from Thursday. Your Veterans' Service Officer will write a note with the salient facts that I can take with me to the appointment. I am so grateful to have him advocate for us.

January 20, 2022

We drove an hour away for your appointment for the cognitive exam only to find it was cancelled. The clinic called your old cell phone number. Another frustrating experience.

January 23, 2022

I asked you to shovel the driveway (got rid of the snow blower because I thought it was too dangerous). I heard you struggle to get into the house. As I opened the door, you fell onto your side. I called 911. The ambulance came. In the hospital, they gave you an IV because you were dehydrated. Your heart rate was slow, so they put a Holter monitor on you. It had to stay on for 48 hours. I thought, good luck with that. All those wires.

January 25, 2022

I took the Holter back.

January 26, 2022

The hospital called. The reading from the Holter was unclear and inconsistent. I was not surprised. The wires on the Holter either fell off or you pulled them off. I said we will not try that again.

Urinary accidents continued. I now concluded your brain cannot communicate with your bladder anymore. I guess this had been obvious for a long time, but I hoped it would get better. It will not.

January 27, 2022

Your primary doctor referred you to a cardiologist.

February 23, 2022

The appointment with the cardiologist will be March 1st. The husband of a friend who also has Alzheimer's Disease had two eerily similar incidents called Syncope's which is a temporary loss of consciousness. He was taken off Aricept because it can cause heart problems. I called your primary doctor, and he said to stop it.

We had our tax return prepared, and you were able to sign your name.

You put your shoes on the wrong feet again. I am trying hard to be patient and am not always successful. You would hate the "new" you.

March 15, 2022

The heart monitor was put in today, and you are leaving it alone. No wires. Just a small device attached to the chest, equipped with a battery. There are two batteries because they need to be charged every day. The device constantly transmits heart rhythms to the cardiologist's office. The cardiologist recommended the heart monitor because you have an abnormally slow heart rate and because of the near-Syncope incidents. Sometimes your breathing is not smooth. You inhale sharply and then sigh loudly. When I ask you if something is wrong, you can't tell me.

March 23, 2022

We saw a VA psychiatrist in Milwaukee today. Her findings determine if you qualify for the disability pension. It will be one to three months until we learn if you will be awarded benefits. I did most of the talking. When the psychiatrist asked you what your favorite food is, you talked about being in the backyard and helping put out a fire. Where did that come from? I miss having lucid conversations with you.

April 18, 2022

You tried to eat dog biscuits and had trouble figuring out how to use a knife. You didn't remember your parents' names and cannot recognize them in a picture. People with Alzheimer's Disease often can remember things from a long time ago but have no recent memories; I don't think you have either.

I made the decision to sell the house as the time is approaching when I will not be able to care for you anymore without sacrificing my own health. First, I need to find a place for me. Every day, I contact the manager of the apartment complex where I want to live about availability.

The heart monitor went back last Thursday. Nothing from the cardiologist about results yet.

VA disability benefits were denied. Your Veterans Service Officer will appeal. He found a Canadian study linking a history of migraines with developing Alzheimer's. A long shot, I thought.

May 3, 2022

No abnormalities were found from the heart monitoring report.

You are very slow getting going in the morning and need help dressing every day. This past week you had urinary accidents every day. My stress level is high. You continued crying in the afternoon and saying, "I am no good. I'm stupid." It is so sad and unbearable. I started a workshop called Powerful Tools for Caregivers offered by the Aging and Disability Resource Center.

The VA is still working on the appeal. That will take months because it is notoriously slow. Bureaucracy.

May 7, 2022

I put the stool in the tub for you to sit on while taking a shower. I thought you could use the shower sprayer, but when I sprayed your head, you freaked out. I do not think you understood where the water was coming from.

May 14, 2022

Got the paperwork regarding the exam for the appeal. It will be a phone call.

June 2, 2022

I received a grant for respite care for you, so I can spend a week at the cottage. On May 16, I had a very brief telephone call with the guy who is a consultant for the VA. He was unaware of the Canadian study and didn't seem to care. He wanted to know how long the migraines persisted after you were discharged from the Navy. I could not tell him, of course, because I did not know you then. I told him I didn't meet you until 1983. It was a useless call.

You tried eating uncooked pasta and a suet cake (used to feed the birds). You ripped out pages again from a book about the national parks. I got angry because I had just put it back together. I yelled at you. Then you started to cry, and I felt awful. I hugged you and apologized for yelling. Why do you tear apart books? I suppose you don't know either. Boredom? Nothing makes sense anymore. The disease is raging in your brain.

It is so unfair. Alzheimer's took our retirement away. We wanted to take a Viking cruise. I am angry at the disease.

June 3, 2022

Today, I am grateful for good friends, the beautiful day, my good health, for you not having an accident at adult daycare, and for spring flowers.

June 4, 2022

You talk a lot in your sleep. Last night, you sang "Happy Birthday" to your brother. Is your memory working when you sleep?

June 5, 2022

The urinary accidents continue. My family continues to offer unsolicited advice about me selling the house, budgets, etc. However, I am grateful for having a family who cares even if they are annoying.

June 29, 2022

It has been a while since I wrote in my journal. Respite care was from June 20-27. While I was at the cottage, you did very well at a memory care facility. A great relief. Once I knew you were doing okay, I was able to relax. One of the residents took you under his wing.

Now we are back home with a new behavior: I am having trouble getting you to take your pills before bedtime. You hold them in your mouth for a second and then spit them out. The crying continues in the afternoon. Are you depressed? I am getting closer to the decision that you would be better cared for in a memory care facility. That, however, requires pots of money. Money—always at the back of my mind.

July 13, 2022

Difficulty giving meds continues. I am now crushing the larger pills and putting them in ice cream so you will take them. Today, you ate a raw potato. I called Consumer Cellular and asked them to disable your cell phone. You will never use it again. I received another grant for respite care. This will be from August 12th through August 18th. I made the decision to put the house on the market. The realtor thinks it will sell fast. I donated your tuxedos, cummerbunds, bow ties, and tuxedo shirts to the Community Clothes Closet. The end of an era. You and I loved ballroom dancing. I kept your beautiful silk ties.

July 25, 2022

I took you to the ER because your balance was unsteady. Bloodwork and a CT scan were negative. The ER doctor said Wellbutrin was the culprit and told me to wean you off it. Your gait was shuffling, and you leaned forward. I was afraid you were going to fall when we went on walks with Jack.

August 9, 2022

Your balance seems better. We did get a walker, but you don't need it now. At least it is here if you ever need it in the future. Your crying in the afternoon continues, which is upsetting. My garage sale was successful. I will be signing the lease on the apartment tomorrow.

August 10, 2022

I signed the lease today. Start date will be October 14th. I will contact the realtor to sign the paperwork to sell the house. It has been a long journey. However, it felt good having decided. I am so fortunate to have received the grants for respite care.

August 19, 2022

I signed the contract with the realtor. A photographer will take pictures of the house. The realtor told me they prefer a sunny day with fluffy clouds. I need to get the house in shape.

August 23, 2022

I took down all the family pictures today. They are a no-no when showing a house. Buyers are supposed to be able to picture their families living there.

August 27, 2022

My niece and her husband brought their trailer, and we hauled away junk to the landfill. My sister and her partner helped me clean the house. It has been exhausting getting the house ready to sell.

You have been wanting to go outside by yourself. I am afraid you will walk away and get lost. I can't blame you for being annoyed at me since I tell you what to do and not to do. What adult likes that? But it is necessary because I worry you will do something that is dangerous.

September 9, 2022

The house went on the market on Friday, September 2nd, and I had an offer by Tuesday. The buyer waived a home inspection, radon testing, and a survey. The settlement will be on October 21st. I don't have to meet the buyer since the realtor will bring the paperwork to sign to me. Your son is coming the first weekend in October for the Alzheimer's Walk.

September 22, 2022

The movers will come on October 19th. I received another two-week respite grant to place you in memory care while I pack for the physical move.

October 1, 2022

Alzheimer's Walk—The day started out cool and later in the morning turned hot. Toward the end of the walk, you were exhausted, probably because you didn't drink enough water. It was a good turnout.

October 17, 2022

I took you to the memory care facility. It is best for both of us for you to stay there permanently. My well has gone dry. The nurse at the facility will need to do an assessment of how much care you need.

October 21, 2022

I moved into the apartment with tremendous help from my niece, sister, her partner, and the movers. This was the worst week of my life, full of conflicting emotions: profound sadness, guilt, relief, and anger. I had a meltdown in church on Sunday. I couldn't stop crying. After the service, the pastor said, "You look like you need a hug," and I did.

Yesterday, I wrote a check for $7,450. The rate is $5,200 per month for the room plus the cost of care of $2,250 which is determined by the amount of assistance individuals need in their daily activities of living, such as help with dressing or undressing, bathing, oral hygiene, eating, toileting, walking, and taking medications. You are at level two. There are four levels. As the disease progresses individuals need more help, and the cost of care increases. Rent increases every January, too. Unless the caregiver has long term insurance, there is a significant drain on the caregiver's financial resources. Many care facilities are not accepting Medical Assistance because of the low reimbursement rates from the government.

I hung pictures in your room. The staff seems nice. The visiting policy is liberal. You are doing okay. You didn't realize that you had not seen me for a couple of weeks.

Jack has adjusted to his new digs. There are many dogs in the complex. I think you would have liked living here. There is a swimming pool, and I know you would have chatted with people while you lounged around the pool.

I miss you very much. I know this is permanent. Being a caregiver was overwhelming, difficult, and stressful. I know you love me, and I love you. Even though you are in a care facility, I remind myself that I am still a caregiver because of the following:

I am the advocate for you because you cannot do that for yourself.

I visit on a regular basis and watch for behavioral changes.

I still do things the staff is too busy to do—cutting your fingernails and shaving your face.

I provide the bed for the room and decorate the room with pictures and other keepsakes that were important to you. I want it to be cozy and welcoming.

I buy clothing, shoes, towels, washcloths, toothpaste and toothbrushes, sheets, pillows, pillowcases, blanket, bedspread, mattress cover, clothes basket, shower gel, body lotion, and incontinence supplies. Fortunately, the staff does the laundry. In other words, I provide every-thing except toilet paper. The facility buys that.

I am responsible for all medical expenses for which Medicare doesn't pay.

I am responsible for ALL bills.

And I must take care of myself.

October 29, 2022

What else could happen this week? First Shingles (got that nipped in the bud because I have had it before), then COVID. I am taking Paxlovid, so I should get better quickly. My symptoms are mild. I can't see you until I test negative for COVID.

November 2, 2022

You tested positive for COVID but are asymptomatic. You were caught eating pudding in the kitchen. The kitchen is off limits to the residents.

November 5, 2022

You tested negative, but I still tested positive. Getting retested tomorrow.

November 8, 2022

I tested negative on Saturday. You are talking again even though you don't make sense. You are sedentary and are putting on weight. The staff suggested a larger size of Depends. We are getting our haircut today. The salon is across the street from Costco (the cheapest place to get Depends).

December 6, 2022

You continue to do well. You were with us on Thanksgiving and will be for Christmas. It is lonely living alone. I miss you.

You tell me I am a good person, and you don't want anything to happen to me. You never ask if you can go home. That is good. I have heard other residents say they want to go home, so I am grateful you have adjusted to living there. It is your home now.

December 12, 2022

I can't help wishing for our life before Alzheimer's, but, of course, that is not going to happen. You say, "I really like you." I say, "I am your wife, and you are my husband." You do not understand the concept of marriage anymore. I ask you to ride the recumbent stair stepper. Muscle memory takes over. Before the disease was evident, we would go to the Y five or six times a week.

December 13, 2022

We saw your primary doctor today. He took a biopsy of a suspicious growth on your head. You tolerated it well. I hope it will not be squamous basal cell carcinoma, which you had earlier in the year. It will take a week to get the results.

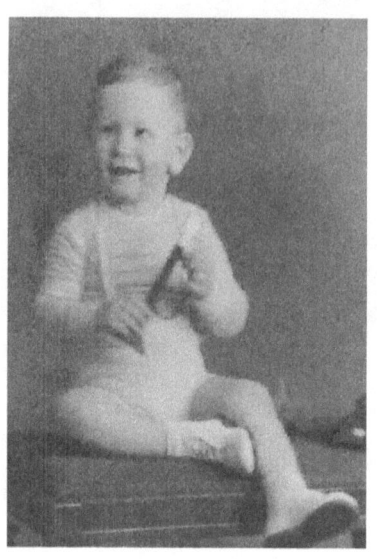

circa 1945

1963 and 1969, respectively

Paul and his son, Eric
circa early 1980s

New Year's Eve, 1987

Paul, siblings, and parents at their 50th wedding anniversary celebration, 1992

Paul and Eric whitewater rafting in California, May 2004

Eric and Jillian's wedding, July 16, 2005

Family cottage

Paul hamming it up at Big Hills Lake, 2007

Chris, Paul, and Eric
Timber Rattlers Game, May 2021

Chris and Paul at cottage
Summer 2021

Paul on his boat

Eric, Jillian, and Indie
Alzheimer's Walk
Santa Monica, California, 2024

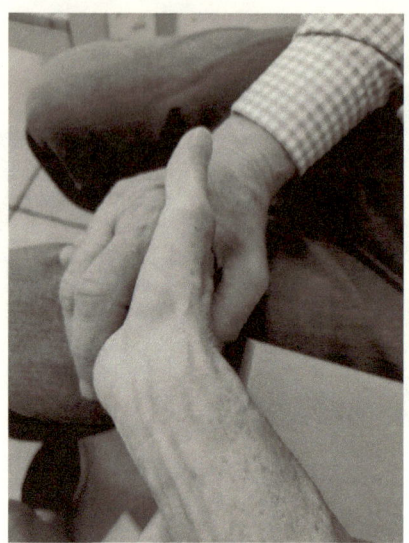

Holding hands, Summer 2023

The red rose in this bouquet dried perfectly from the bouquet
at Paul's Memorial Service, January 20, 2024

December 20, 2022

It was not cancer, but your doctor removed the growths on your head, and you did well with that.

December 25, 2022

Christmas

You stayed with me last night because the weather was so awful, below zero temperatures. I was afraid to take you back to the facility. The roads were hazardous. You talked in your sleep and wet the bed. I didn't sleep well worrying that you might do that. I held your hand while we slept. I believe this will be the last time I will sleep with you.

In the morning, I did a stupid thing. I gave you a bath, and when you were done, you could not figure out how to get out of the tub. It was as if your legs and arms were made of Jello. You used to be such a strong person. I had to call 911. I didn't tell my family because I was embarrassed.

In hindsight, I believe you would have been better off staying at the facility, but I didn't want you to be alone on Christmas. I knew other residents would be with their families. Will this be our last Christmas together?

January 1, 2023

I found you sitting next to one of the residents with her glasses on your face and yours in her pocket.

January 10, 2023

I am increasingly concerned about your weight gain. I asked if dessert at lunch could be withheld. They said no because it is a resident's right to have dessert. When you were placed there, you wore size 34 jeans, you are now size 38. You will eat whatever is put before you. You don't recognize when you are full, I think. I continue to get you on the recumbent, and we walk around the hallways. Your room faces the parking lot, and you like to look outside at the cars in the parking lot and people coming and going.

January 28, 2023

We have a compromise. The facility is now giving you diabetic desserts, eliminating fruit juices, and not giving you a second plate of food. Having a sweet tooth you don't care what dessert you get, just that you get something. You continue to be contented.

February 19, 2023

I saw you today and wasn't sure if you knew me. You do not know my sister. One of the staff said you talk and laugh in the middle of the night when she goes to change you. Strange because you rarely talk during the day.

February 23, 2023

The facility called 911 for you today because you collapsed after eating lunch. At the ER, you violently vomited three times. Dehydrated again. X-rays showed a bowel obstruction. When I left at 9 PM, the ER doctor was going to insert a gastro nasal tube, standard protocol for someone with a bowl obstruction. I told him you would pull it out, which you did. For two days food was withheld, and the bowel obstruction resolved on its own. I was so happy surgery was not necessary.

While you were there, a Statement of Mental Incompetency was executed by two physicians which supersedes an executed Power of Attorney for Healthcare. Also, a Do Not Resuscitate order was put in place even though you are wearing a DNR bracelet.

February 27, 2023

You were released today. You have a follow-up appointment with your doctor and with the cardiologist. I sure hope this doesn't happen again.

March 6, 2023

You saw the cardiologist's physician's assistant. The plan is to insert an Implantable Loop Recorder (heart monitor) to help determine if you need a pacemaker.

March 15, 2023

Approval for the loop recorder came through. I took Jack to see you today. He liked seeing you and getting pats from other residents. However, you ignored him. We walked the hallways, and Jack was good when you were on the recumbent. The Depends no longer work. At the request of the facility, I now order heavy duty adult diapers on-line for you. According to them, you are a "heavy wetter."

March 29, 2023

I haven't seen you since last Tuesday because of a nasty intestinal bug at the facility. You were quite ill.

March 31, 2023

The virus is gone, so I saw you today.

April 9, 2023

Easter

I picked up you at 11:30 AM. Again, I did not think you knew your family. I drove you back at 5:30 PM. You are slipping away quickly. I am losing my love.

April 11, 2023

The pastor came to see you today. While you rode the recumbent, we talked. I told her about a recent dream I had about you. You landed a controller job with a large corporation. We were both thrilled because you found meaningful work again. She said, "You are looking for a miracle." With Alzheimer's, miracles are not possible. As she was leaving, you told her she was a nice person. You tell this to most people.

April 23, 2023

You had the Implantable Loop Recorder procedure last Thursday. You did remarkably well. The cardiologist did not want to sedate you because of dementia, so he numbed the area with Lidocaine and inserted the small device under the skin. No stitches. Just a couple of Steri Strips with a gauze pad on top. I set up the monitoring device on the nightstand near your bed. The device constantly transmits the heart rhythms to the monitoring center. You don't even know it's there.

May 11, 2023

You continue to be sad. One of the staff thought you cry when you are wet. I don't know, but it breaks my heart. We sat outside on the lovely terrace, a flowering oasis. You seem to like being outside and watching the river.

May 19, 2023

We played bingo with others. You won once; my sister won once; I won once. I had to help you with the Bingo card. You did not recognize the numbers and fell asleep. You liked the prize, a piece of candy. Your weight has stabilized, and the incision healed well.

May 21, 2023

While playing bingo today, you put a poker chip in your mouth twice. Fortunately, you didn't try to swallow it. Alarming, nevertheless. Toddler-like behavior. But that's what happens with Alzheimer's.

May 23, 2023

Today is our 31st wedding anniversary, but we have been together for 40 years. You didn't remember, of course.

June 14, 2023

We sat on the terrace. You fell asleep muttering to yourself. I couldn't understand what you said. Your son and his family are coming this weekend.

June 21, 2023

Your son and his family were here last weekend. They live in California. They arrived late Thursday evening and left Sunday morning. On Friday morning, I went with your son to see you. On Saturday and Sunday, your son went alone. Our granddaughter swam in the complex's pool—quite the little swimmer. When I asked your son about how he found you, he said he was prepared for your decline. He keeps his cards close to his chest.

June 30, 2023

The connection between us is going away. Do you know me? Sometimes unexpectedly you will say my name.

There is a saying; "the eyes are the window to the soul." When I look into your eyes now, I see blankness.

I shave you with an electric razor because a straight razor bothers you. You are reluctant to wash your hands. Alzheimer's changes the brain, so water hitting the skin can feel like pins and needles to some people with the disease.

You like your hands held. Touch makes you feel secure. You still give the best hugs. Your kisses are chaste.

You don't talk much, and when you do, you talk so softly I have a tough time hearing you.

I showed you a picture of our great grandniece. You touched the screen on my phone. Did you know how important this person would become to you?

I used to feel compelled to see you every day. You don't realize when I don't come, but I need to take time for myself without feeling guilty.

Alzheimer's is truly a slow death. Every caregiver grieves each day. The hardest thing for me is not knowing when the disease will release its grip on you. I found it difficult to let go of the man I married and to accept that person is permanently gone. People do not recover from Alzheimer's.

You don't know you have a son. You do not recognize his picture.

With Alzheimer's, there are many "never agains." You will never know your granddaughter or your great niece's daughter. You will never go on a plane or go to the cottage again. You will never remember what Christmas, Thanksgiving, Easter, or Valentine's Day mean. You will never remember our anniversary or my birthday or your own birthday.

Occasionally, I will get a smile from you, and that makes my day. You smiled after our hairdresser cut your hair when she told you how handsome you are. She comes to the facility now.

July 2, 2023

I went to the cottage for a week. When I came back, I went to see you. They had not shaved you. You looked scruffy. I know they are busy. You must have scratched the end of your nose because there was a big scab.

We had tomato soup and a grilled cheese sandwich for lunch. You had Jello for dessert.

We sat outside for a while. It was a sweltering day, in the 90s. You fell asleep. You didn't seem very alert today. One of the residents died last week. He was your friend and a nice man.

July 6, 2023

I woke up after two hours of sleeping last night with these words in my head, and I had to get them out.

Recently, while I was eating lunch with you, I looked out the windows and saw a guy sculling on the river. He went under the bridge and rowed into the inlet. I mentioned this to a friend who is also a rower, and she said it would have been difficult for him to get to the inlet because it is very rocky and shallow under the bridge. A good analogy for our lives—full of obstacles. In other words, the ravages of Alzheimer's Disease on your brain. You are, fortunately, now oblivious to these obstacles, unlike a couple of years ago.

In 2019, before you were diagnosed with Alzheimer's, I remember you saying: "I am doing the best I can." I knew you were struggling then.

I have a picture on my phone of you and me taken in 2021. I showed it to a member of the staff yesterday, she remarked on the difference in your appearance between 2021 and 2023.

You were sad tonight, crying; for what reason, you can't tell me why. I don't know what to do to comfort you, other than to hold your hand. Then, just like that, you get over it and smile. The staff tells me this has been happening frequently of late. I wonder how it will be when I visit you again.

July 8, 2023

You have been here ten months. Eating has changed again. You have trouble figuring out what utensil to use. If you have a sandwich, you take it apart and eat each part separately.

My feeling is the staff wants to include you in activities, but you don't care and keep yourself apart from the others. So, unlike the man I married who was a social animal.

July 16, 2023

The other day, I observed you playing noodle ball. The residents sat in a circle and hit a small balloon with a noodle. The objective was to keep it in the air. You didn't understand you should throw the balloon in the air and hit it with the noodle. Instead, you hit the balloon as if you were playing baseball. That was okay. At least, you participated part of the time. You had a smile on your face.

We sat on the patio today for half an hour. You fell asleep and were talking to yourself. You started to bend forward. I was afraid you were going to fall off your chair. I took you back inside. We walked around. You called me by my name, so I know you still remember me. You were in your own world today.

July 20, 2023

From 10 AM to noon today, the facility was pre-fundraising for the Alzheimer's Walk on October 8th. I bought purple wristbands, one for me and four for family members.

I found you outside by the fire pit. The staff had already taken you for a walk. Since it was a beautiful day, not too hot and zero humidity, I took you for another one. We walked along the path by the river.

Before lunch one of the staff brought in her long-haired chihuahua, a cute dog. She told me you liked the dog. She asked you if you wanted to hold it. You didn't. Shrugging, she said: "Guess it is not that kind of a day." That's the way with Alzheimer's. Your loved one can behave differently from one day to the next. Except you know the disease will never release its grip.

Recently, there have been reports in various media outlets about new Alzheimer's drugs approved by the FDA that are supposed to help deter the progression of early onset Alzheimer's. It is too late to help you, but if they help slow down the progression of the disease for people recently diagnosed, that is good. Alzheimer's is an evil disease.

August 1, 2023

I went to see you today after being gone for a week. Unlike the previous time I went away, the staff had shaved you. You looked well and seemed happy to see me. We ate lunch together. I cut your fingernails because the staff does not have time to do so. You are biting the nails on your left hand.

Last week, while I was at the cottage, one of the staff called to tell me you tried to eat a wooden block. Why? Were you hungry? No damage to your mouth, thank goodness.

August 5, 2023
Your Birthday

You were 78. I brought a delicious cake to share, lemon with raspberry filling, your favorite. It was also another resident's birthday. Someone asked me if I made the cake, and I said no. It was a great hit. After reading your birthday cards to you, I put them on your dresser in your room.

My sister and her partner came. It was a beautiful day, and we sat outside on the patio again. After three and a half hours, I left. I hope you had a good rest of your day. We always had great birthday parties at the cottage, not only for you but for the others who had summer birthdays. I miss those celebrations.

August 16, 2023

I haven't written since your birthday on Augusts 5th. When our grandniece came to see you last month, she hadn't seen you since 2019 when you were still communicative. She cried, astonished at your decline. I was expecting that because she loves you very much. Even I am stunned at how quickly you have changed. How long will the holding pattern last? Good people kindly tell me God has a plan, and I should trust in that. I don't know if that is true. I just see reality. Shit happens, and there is nothing you can do about it.

I have asked the facilitators of my support group to talk about "anticipatory grief." I think the discussion could be useful.

August 17, 2023

I am slowly finding out former occupations of some of the residents. Regardless of education, cultural standing, or service to others, dementia does not discriminate.

August 30, 2023

Today, I came home from a week's stay at the cottage. There are vestiges of your presence at the cottage over the years—carefully coded food containers (cover and container marked with the
same code) for ease of putting away leftovers—pier poles and wooden sections marked, so we know what section goes in first in the spring—the edges of the slate steps going down to the lake painted white. When there were many people at the cottage, you organized the food in the fridge. Disorder was disturbing to you. You cleaned out and organized the storage shed and the boathouse. You *always* found something to do when you were there.

"Straightening things out" gave you great satisfaction. Now your brain is a battle zone. The disease has created disorder by destroying the natural order of your brain.

I will see you tomorrow. I am sure you will not remember I have been gone for a week, but that doesn't matter because it is what it is, and there is nothing I can do about it.

September 5, 2023

I was talking to a staff member in your presence the other day. We talked as if you weren't there. That got me thinking. Obviously, you can't easily follow a quick conversation, but can you understand anything at all that was spoken? Most people would not think about talking about their spouse's private matters to another person if their spouse could hear the conversation. Alzheimer's gives you that permission.

After supper tonight, I was walking Jack, and an older couple passed us, similar in age to you and me. They were talking and laughing. My first reaction was jealousy. Life is so unfair. Enough said. I wish there were something I could do to take away this pain of losing you.

September 20, 2023

As I was walking Jack, I stopped to greet a woman who was walking her son's dog, a friend of Jack's. She and her husband belong to our old church. We started talking, and I told her what was happening in my life. She talked about her father, who had dementia, and her mother who cared for her father. Her mother died of cancer. She said she had no doubt the stress of being a caregiver contributed to her mother's death.

Anyway, she said something which gave me pause: "This time with your husband is sacred." She is correct because who knows how much time is left with you? Time with you should not be squandered.

In fact, every day should be sacred for each of us as we never know what life is going to throw at us. Today was a good day when I visited you. You were alert, and you said my name. Every day is different. A roller coaster experience.

When I went to see you today, I hugged you, as usual. You looked at me and kissed me on the cheek. A first since you have been there. You made my day.

September 24, 2023

Just a brief note today. I watched the first half of the Packer's game, your favorite football team, They were not playing well, so I went to see you. Before you got sick, you had perfect football acumen. After all, you were a champion quarterback when you were in high school. You could always see a penalty as it happened. No longer. You no longer know which team to cheer for.

After walking around for a while, we were sitting in comfy chairs, and one of the ladies who is still semi-aware asked if she could take our picture. She said she could take it with my phone if I showed her how to do it. It didn't work out, but that doesn't matter. It was the kind gesture that mattered. As she frequently does, she complimented you on being handsome and such a gentleman and remarked how loyal I am by being there every day. Then she said this must be so hard on you. I concurred.

October 11, 2023

I went to my support group this afternoon. We talked about making tough decisions for the care of your loved one. Your family might not like it, but your loved one would want you to make those decisions. A suggestion from one of the facilitators: Keep a notebook by your bed. If you are awakened in the middle of the night, you can write down your thoughts.

October 12, 2023

Today I spent the afternoon at the ER with you at the behest of the staff. They were concerned because you were extremely weak. They had trouble getting you out of bed at night to take you to the bathroom. Lately I noticed you have difficulty sitting down and standing up. Your walking is wobbly.

Diagnostic tests were done—no infections, the chest X-ray normal. The CT scan of your head showed vascular damage. You were a little dehydrated again. They gave you an IV. The ER doctor said you could have had a minor stroke, but we would not know that unless he admitted you and put you through a battery of tests that would make you uncomfortable and even more confused. He and I did not want to do that. Back you went to the facility. I am confident they will take good care of you. My gut tells me the disease has progressed even more rapidly.

October 13, 2023, 1 AM

Trouble sleeping tonight. When we had to put down our previous dog, my niece said, "You have given him a gift," meaning we were eliminating his suffering. Yesterday, when the ER doctor did not want to admit you and subject you to unnecessary tests that was a *gift* to me. I thanked him for his kindness and empathy. Being on this journey has given me more strength, more resilience, more assertiveness, and, most importantly, more kindness.

October 16, 2023

What Is Anticipatory Grief? It is grief that occurs before a loss and is common among caregivers. When you have a loved one with dementia, you grieve every day. You want the "old" person to come back, but he or she won't, as you intellectually know. I had never heard of the term anticipatory grief until I found myself in the situation I am in now. Will it help when the end comes? Perhaps.

October 26, 2023

What a difference a day makes. Yesterday, you smiled and called me by my name. Today was different. Again, you had trouble standing up and sitting down and walking. One staff member told me you winced as if being in pain when she put your right shoe on. You rub your right knee frequently. The staff and I feel your right knee or right leg hurts. Osteoarthritis? I contacted your doctor, and he ordered Tylenol. In dealing with Alzheimer's, caregivers need to be detectives, not an easy task.

October 31, 2023

Last week Thursday, I was at the facility and saw a resident who was in throes of death. He was in his wheelchair. I had never seen an individual who was on the verge of "crossing over." He was 95 years old, and his time had come. The staff took him to his room.

Friday, I left for a women's retreat an hour away. The theme was mindfulness.

I often go about my day without thinking about the elements in my environment. Imagine you were taking a walk on an early spring morning. Did you see the white fluffy cumulus clouds in the beautiful blue sky? Were you aware of the green shoots of spring plants sprouting from the earth? Did you hear bird songs? Could you identify the bird calls? Did you feel the sun's warmth on your skin? If you were going past a pond, did you hear the spring peepers? Did you smell newly mown grass? Mindfulness is not easy, and I make feeble attempts to practice it. It was nice to get away on a gorgeous fall weekend and to be with a group of interesting women.

I saw you on Monday. You were still weak and had difficulty sitting down and standing up. One of the staff who was doing an activity talked about the resident dying and how there was a ceremony to honor the person who died. I was moved by that.

I bought you four shirts, size large, and took the too-small shirts away. You have gained about 20 pounds since you moved there. However, I understand food is the only pleasure you have. It is hard to see a vigorous, extremely fit person gone. The physical therapist is coming tomorrow afternoon. PT is to keep you from having to be in a wheelchair.

November 1, 2023

I did not see you today. In a text message your physical therapist told me you were in a wheelchair when she arrived. She had you stand up and sit down ten times to strengthen your quads. You used the recumbent. She hopes you might turn around soon. I am not so sure.

November 2, 2023

You were not in a wheelchair today. I was able to get you to sit down in a chair and stand up a couple of times. We walked around the hallways. You did not use the recumbent because I was afraid you were too weak and lately you have been having difficulty getting off of it. I sent a message to your primary physician who felt we may be at the point where physical therapy will not help much due to the rapidly progressing disease.

November 3, 2023

You were back in the wheelchair today. At the request of the staff, I spent the afternoon in the ER again with you. They thought the increased weakness in your legs and increased confusion might be caused by a UTI. They were not. All the tests were normal.

It took two people to get you in and out of my small car. You had trouble bending your head to get into the car, sitting down, and getting your knees into the vehicle. If there is another ER visit in the future, you will have to be transported by the facility's van.

Next Tuesday I have an appointment with your primary doctor to discuss palliative care or hospice care. I had thought hospice care was for a person close to death. Not true. According to the staff, there are several people at your facility who have been in hospice for quite a while.

November 4, 2023

While pushing you around for a while, one of the residents came out with a power bar. I broke off a piece for you to eat. Then, she brought out a small glass of water saying you needed it. The power bar is dry.

While we were "walking" around, she was sweeping the floors. I told her that wasn't her job, but she said she was one of 13 children and knew how to clean. She was bored. She was a registered nurse for 35 years. From all appearances, one would think she did not belong there, but I was told by the staff every resident is there for a reason. She told my sister she has Alzheimer's. Every day, she does crosswords and Sudoku.

November 7, 2023

You were in a wheelchair from Thursday to Monday but not today. Alzheimer's is fickle, daily ups and downs.

November 8, 2023

I placed you in hospice, a tough decision but the right one. This was news to me. A person cannot be in physical therapy and hospice at the same time because the goals are different. PT is to help a person get better, and hospice is to keep the person comfortable. I made the difficult decision to ask your physician about your life expectancy. While you had been holding your own for a while, there had been sudden, significant declines. He said he is not clairvoyant, but going by his past experiences with other patients, he thought your life expectancy was a few months. He said most people with Alzheimer's die of pneumonia.

Your physician will no longer see you in person. The hospice RN will be the liaison between the doctor, the facility, and myself. I met with her two days ago. She will come two days a week, and a Certified Nursing Assistant will come three times a week. Hospice provides supplemental care to what the staff provides, such as fingernail and toenail cutting, a massage once a month, pet therapy, music therapy, and emotional support for me. There is a social worker assigned to the case. Hospice purchases all supplies, including incontinence products. The hospice nurses monitor medications, change bed linens, help with showering, dressing, and brushing teeth. Hospice also supplies medical equipment.

To qualify for hospice, the individual must have a terminal illness and will be reevaluated at three months and six months to see if there have been declines in the condition of the patient. The RN looks for changes in personality, such as suddenly yelling, having difficulty using silverware, or starting to sleep more. You already spend most of the day sleeping.

I am cognizant you are embarking on the last leg of this journey we have been on since 2018, and I am sure it started earlier than that.

November 15, 2023

I think I heard you speak my name today, but you speak
so softly now, I have a hard time hearing you.

November 16, 2023

Today at lunch you had a bib. It had a pocket, so food wouldn't fall on the floor. Why did it take them so long to figure this out? The CNA gave you a shower this morning. You looked nice. You had on a new blue and white checked flannel shirt I bought you and new pants.

November 18, 2023

Today was a good day. When I arrived, you smiled at me and gave me a kiss. You were also without your wheelchair again. Go figure? We walked around quite a bit. I ate lunch with you, and you fed yourself with your fork. Unlike yesterday, you were alert. As I have said before, every day is different.

November 19, 2023

It is funny how observations can cause sadness. I was in church today sitting next to a well-dressed guy. He had a suit on and a crisp blue shirt sans tie. I looked at his shoes and remembered how important it was for you to look good when you went to church. You had beautiful shoes, beautiful clothing, and gorgeous ties. I haven't gotten rid of everything of yours because it is upsetting to do so. Someone may ask why? He will never wear them again. They are just clothes. But they represent the guy you used to be. The guy who always looked good, except for those gold U of Michigan sweatpants that I finally threw away because they had huge holes in them. Without you, it is not the same and never will be.

Left are two cashmere top coats, a raincoat, your dress hats, your Navy jacket with your name on the pocket, a winter vest, winter boots, winter gloves, a couple of dress shoes, three suits (I have already given away 25), dress shirts, your bathrobe, and lots and lots of ties.

November 20, 2023

I met the CNA this morning. She said a larger wheel-chair would be more comfortable for you. It will allow you to lean back and will be easier on your knees. Now, when you fall asleep you lean forward and are in danger of falling out of the chair.

I tried to feed you, but you did not want to eat your lunch today. You took a few bites of the crab cake. I was afraid you were going to choke on your food. You ate the cookie. The whole time you didn't open your eyes. The weird thing is you ate your breakfast by yourself. The staff told me when they got you out of bed in the morning, you didn't want to stand up. It took three people to get you into the wheelchair. Your hospice nurse is going to visit others today, and she will check in on you, too. She also thought you were tired. I will see her tomorrow.

November 21, 2023

Another momentous day today. You were still in bed when I got there. I rubbed your large, beautiful feet which you seemed to like. Your toes are straight, unlike mine that are deformed from arthritis. The hospice nurse said as the disease progresses, people typically sleep more and sometimes won't get out of bed during the day. I witnessed how difficult it is for the staff to get you dressed. You were dead weight, and it took the hospice RN and two staff members to roll you over on your side.

The hospice nurse ordered a Broda wheelchair. Bigger than the typical wheelchair. It has a higher back and more leg room, which accommodates a tall person much better. She also ordered a sling so they can use the Hoya Lift to get you in and out of bed.

After you got up, you ate a peanut butter and jelly sandwich and drank a glass of flavored water.

November 22, 2023

It has been quite a stressful couple of weeks since I placed you in hospice. Today the hospital bed and the wheelchair came. I got up early and went to Target and bought extra-long twin sized sheets, a quilt, a packet of extra-large size undershirts, and another XL shirt.

I took my purchases to your facility, took back all the queen size bedding, went to the madhouse we call Costco, and got my hair cut. The facility took down the queen size bed. I need to remove it. Life is not easy.

November 25, 2023

The day after Thanksgiving, my family helped me get the queen-size bed out of your room. The hospital bed will make it much easier to care for you. While we were doing this, you were eating your breakfast on your own.

In my apartment, we moved the bed into the second bedroom. At first, I wanted it to go into the master bedroom, but it would have been too much work to switch out the beds. I don't mind the queen-size bed being in the second bedroom. It carries so much history, 36 years. It was our sanctuary where we cherished each other, reminisced, and had discussions about our future. On a sour note, it also was where the incontinence first manifested itself. I do not want to sleep in it every night.

November 26, 2023

I am feeling frustrated because I can't find on TV any of my favorite Christmas movies that bring me comfort, other than *Love Actually*, which I have already rewatched for the umpteenth time. Plus, Netflix and Amazon Prime are not coming in tonight. Not sure what is wrong.

Yesterday and today, I had lunch with you. Saturday, yesterday, you had a huge breakfast, so you weren't too hungry at lunch. Today, I had to prompt you to use your fork. You ate very, very slowly and didn't finish all your lunch, including the delicious chocolate chip cookie. You love cookies.

Afterwards, I tried to push you around in the new wheelchair. It was difficult because you won't keep your feet on the footrests. We went back to your room. The hospice nurse often said people with a terminal illness will hang on to life because of concern for their loved ones. She said it was okay for me to give you permission to let go.

While you were awake, I did so. I took your hands and tried to assure you I would survive without you, no matter how much I will miss you and will be lonely without you. I acknowledged to you I knew you hated living this way. You couldn't verbalize that, but I am sure you felt that way deep down in your soul. I assured you I would always love you. You were a person with so much joie de vie.

December 1, 2023

Yesterday I went to a funeral home to plan and pre-pay for your memorial service. The hospice nurse said it was a good idea, one less thing to think about when the time comes.

My sister came with me, and your son participated in the meeting via Zoom. He said he wanted time to talk about his dad at the end of the service, and I knew there would be other family members who would also wish to talk about how you touched their hearts throughout the years. I wanted to make the service personal—to focus on the person who affected so many lives. He asked about music, and I told him I wanted "Amazing Grace" in the beginning and "The Wind Beneath My Wings" at the end of the service before military rites. There were two poems about Alzheimer's that I wanted read by the English poet, Donna Ashworth, the 23rd Psalm, and the Lord's Prayer. The pastor will finalize the order of service.

I went to see you in the afternoon. You were back to rubbing your right knee. In pain or just a habit? You shouldn't be in pain since you are on Tramadol twice a day. The CNA suggested a "fidget blanket." Below is a picture of one. They are lap blankets that have items sewn on top of the blanket, such as buttons, or beads, or keys. Volunteers make them. It allows Alzheimer's patients to do something with their hands. I thought it was an interesting concept. They will bring one for you soon. We will see if you like it.

I took the rest of your clothing to the Community Close Closet today. (I still have the ties. A friend could make a pillow from them.

December 2, 2023

In the morning, I went to a Christmas brunch. Afterwards, I went to see you. There was an activity going on. I pulled up a chair and sat next to you. As usual, you were sleeping. For the first time, I felt rejected by you. I always held your hand when we sat next to each other. However, you shoved my hand away. I knew I shouldn't take it personally. It is the disease.

Also, yesterday I brought your wedding ring back to you, thinking you would leave it alone. Today I noticed it was not on your finger. In the middle of the night, staff found you chewing on it. They were afraid you were either going to chip a tooth or choke on it. Disappointed, I took it home.

Lunch was soup, a biscuit, and dessert. Because you have difficulty grasping a spoon, eating soup is hard. Instead of the soup going into your mouth, most of it ends up on your shirt. I asked for a bib and a cup. I fed you. When lunch was over, I took you to your room. I sat with you for a while. You took my hand and rubbed your knee with it. I hate this disease. It is cruel.

December 5, 2023

I went to see you early this morning, 9:30 AM, because the hospice nurse was there. She was helping you eat breakfast. I expressed concern that you were isolated from the other residents, and it is impossible to engage with you anymore. I was grateful when she said she would ask hospice volunteers to come and sit with you.

In the morning, I sat with you for four hours in your room today. You slept while I read my book. At lunch, you were able to feed yourself, partly. You ate the chicken salad sandwich without difficulty and drank your water. I helped you eat the cucumber salad. Increasingly now, you are falling asleep when you are eating your lunch.

The hospice nurse also told me she feels you know it is me when I hold your hand. I hope so.

December 9, 2023

Yesterday, the hospice nurse brought the fidget blanket. You like it.

Today's lunch was two pizza slices, salad, and a little bit of a brownie. You ate your lunch by yourself with prompts from me. You continue to fall asleep at lunch.

One staff member told me in the middle of the night, you said out loud you couldn't go grocery shopping anymore. You used to do all the grocery shopping.

December 18, 2023

When I went to see you today after they fed you lunch, I could not wake you up. You stroked my hand while I sat next to you. I had an uneasy feeling. I contacted your hospice nurse. If you weren't better at supper time, she asked me to let the staff know they should call hospice.

The hospice nurse on-call phoned me at 8:30 PM and said your body was shutting down. Your extremities were cold and blue, meaning the heart is not pumping blood well, and your breathing was rapid and shallow. Days to a week before the end. She gave you morphine. You were comfortable, in bed, and would remain there for the remaining time until death. These hospice nurses do not mince words. It was shocking to hear the words. Tomorrow, I planned to speak with your regular hospice nurse.

We had a good life together. I love you to the moon and back. You will finally be released from this cruel and horrible disease.

December 19, 2023

The facility called me at 2:30 AM. The first call came to my cell phone. It was a Georgia number. As I did not know anyone there, I did not answer. Immediately, the landline rang. I rushed to the second bedroom to pick it up. It was the CNA from the facility. She said it was an emergency, and I should come immediately. I asked if you were dying, and she said you were gone.

What? It wasn't supposed to happen tonight. The hospice nurse told me you had a few more days to live. I didn't even get to say a proper goodbye. Why didn't I spend more time with you yesterday? My heart pounded. My pulse raced. My legs wobbled. I had to hold onto the dresser so I wouldn't fall.

My hands trembled as I called my sister. We went to the facility. Because you were in hospice care, we had to wait until the hospice RN on-call came. The CNA said she had never seen anything like this before. Bodily fluids had erupted from your mouth, and they were all over your undershirt. Blood or stomach contents? She and a member of the staff cleaned you up before they allowed us to see you.

One of your shoes was lying at the end of the bed. Lonely without its partner. Where was the mate? I imagined they just tossed your shoes willy-nilly when they got you in bed.

Your mouth was open. I was glad your eyes were closed. When I touched you, your skin was cold, your fingernails blue. I kissed the top of your head and stroked your arm and hand. Our long journey had ended. I was part of a couple for 40 years. My life irrevocably changed forever.

When I spoke to your sister, she said she got up in the middle of the night and saw a cardinal on her deck railing. For many people, cardinals represent a visit from a deceased loved one. She thought it was you.

December 20, 2023

There was a voice message from the heart monitoring center at the cardiologist's office. I returned the call, and the person who was reading last night's report said your heart experienced tachycardia. I told her you passed away. That explained it, she said, and offered me her sincere condolences. Your beautiful and generous heart gave up.

In the morning, my niece and I went to the funeral home for a final discussion with the funeral director. The Memorial Service was set for January 20, 2024. I signed the paperwork authorizing the cremation.

The funeral home was able to make a CD of background music. All I had to do was send a list. The funeral director said they would provide me with a copy of the CD after the service. Also, there would be a video of pictures of you during the service in addition to the picture poster boards.

I decided on the January date because our niece from Washington state was planning to come to see her mother around that time, and your son planned to come to see you the weekend after New Year's to say goodbye. Both were able to change their flights.

In the afternoon, my sister and her daughter, her partner, and I went to the funeral home for a final goodbye. I kissed your left hand and put your wedding ring back on. I wanted you to have it on the final leg of your journey.

In the afternoon, I hauled out a box of pictures and asked my niece and her mother to help me sort through them. I wanted good pictures of you for the display boards at the Memorial Service. My sister frequently said, "Oh, this is an awful picture." Then she proceeded to tear up the picture and to place it in a discard pile. Despite our grief, we laughed because some pictures were truly horrible. Why do we keep awful pictures?

December 21, 2023

I met with the pastor to plan the Order of Service. She showed me bulletins from other funerals at which she officiated and was amenable to whatever I wanted. In the end, I thought the finished product was beautiful. I told the pastor about the cardinal on your sister's deck, and she asked me if I had had any signs of you. I said no.

When I went to clean out your room, staff told me how shocked they were at your sudden death as it was unexpected. You did not exhibit the behavior dying people usually do, such as refusing to eat or drink.

With the help of my sister, her daughter, and movers, we emptied the room quickly. I said goodbye to one of the resident's husbands. He and I had tears in our eyes.

December 31-January 11

I continued to search for pictures. I went back through the box several more times, looked at the pictures on my computer and cell phone, and asked family members if they had any good pictures. I also sent digital pictures to the funeral director for the video. In the end I had enough pictures for four poster boards.

I spent a considerable amount of time finding the background music. The list included a mixture of classical music, popular songs, and a hymn. Those tasks occupied most of my time from the end of December through the first two weeks in January.

I ordered food from Costco for the gathering after the service, probably too much food, but I had no idea how many people would show up.

January 12, 2024

A blizzard was forecasted for this day, and the weather man did not lie. Before the weather got too bad, I walked Jack. Just across the street from my place, I fell on ice hidden under the snow. My left foot went forward. My right foot went backwards with the top of my right foot on the ground. Even though it hurt, I was able to walk back home, so I thought I had sprained it. I called my primary doctor and was told I should be seen that day. The only available appointment was at 10:30 AM, just when the storm would be ramping up. I called my sister and asked if she could take me to the ER.

Just as she arrived, Jack decided to have a panic attack. Usually when that happens, I give him gabapentin to calm him down. No time for that. With the wind howling, we struggled to get into the car. Her windshield wipers were hardly able to keep up with the pelting snow. Because it was too cold to leave Jack in the car, she waited there while I went in. Fortunately, there were no other people in the ER. An x-ray revealed fractured second and third metatarsals in my right foot. They put a boot on my foot and asked me to make an appointment with a podiatrist for evaluation since an injury like this might require surgery.

January 12-18, 2024

Jack and I stayed with my sister and her partner from Friday to Thursday. The whole time, the weather was frigid—minus zero temperatures. I felt awful because my sister's partner had to walk Jack in that horrible, bitter cold, and Jack was not too happy about it, either.

On the 18th, I saw the podiatrist. Fortunately, surgery was not necessary, but I needed to be in the boot for six or seven weeks. Disappointing, but I was glad surgery was not necessary. Tolerating the boot would be difficult and confining because I couldn't drive. In the afternoon of that day, I went back home. Your son arrived via Uber late near midnight.

January 19, 2024

My niece, her husband, and their dog, Rory arrived in the morning. While my niece and I went to buy a bouquet and went out to lunch, your son and my niece's husband went to Costco. In the afternoon, we set up the Community Room in my apartment complex for the gathering after the service. I told your son to bring warm clothes. Nevertheless, he was shocked at how bitterly cold it was.

January 20, 2024

The day of your Memorial Service arrived with bright sun and blue sky. It was still very cold. The sidewalks were icy, and there were piles of snow.

We arrived at the funeral home at 8:30 AM. I put the bouquet and a picture of us on the table in front of the room. Also on the table was a black box containing your ashes and a lit candle with your picture on it.

While family members set up the picture boards, I watched the video of you and cried. I was pleased with how they put together the video. You shined, just like in life, on the picture boards and throughout the video.

I was pleasantly surprised by the number of people who came to pay their respects. The first person who came was the man whom I greeted when we were cleaning out your room. My oldest sister, 89, and her husband, 95, live in Iowa. She wanted to come with her son's family, but the weather was just too frigid. Because your family members live in Pennsylvania, New Hampshire, and Florida, they did not come, but they watched the service via livestream.

The pastor did not know you very well. When I planned the service with her, she asked me questions about you. I mentioned you would often say, "That is not a good way to do that, Christine," if you disagreed with the way I was doing something. Her remarks were titled "The Best Way." She must have read the obituary because she captured your essence very well. Nieces read the two poems. Family members spoke about how you touched their lives and how they will miss you. The service ended with Taps and presentation of the flag by two young sailors.

At the post-service gathering, we had a mini family reunion. Most of us had not seen or spoken with each other in a long while. The five Iowan relatives left with a platter of food.

January 21, 2024

We divided up the leftovers. Part of them went into my freezer, and my niece and her husband took the rest. My niece who lives in Washington went home with her sister. Jack went home with them, too, and your son returned to California. I cried when everyone left. It was so quiet in the apartment. Nobody to talk to. Of course, I understood they had their own lives to live. I was consumed with isolation and desolation. I was facing a long rest of January and February with the boot on. Confined to my apartment because I could not drive and having to depend on others to drive me to appointments.

January 22, 2024

I took all the pictures off the boards.

January 27, 2024

I watched the livestream of Memorial Service and listened to the CD of the background music. Listening to the songs made me cry. Your son told me he watched the livestream twice and was still processing your death.

February 8, 2024

Saw the podiatrist. Three more weeks in the boot. Bummer!

February 19, 2024

Two months since you left us. Still adjusting to that.

February 22, 2024

What can I say about grief? Not anticipatory anymore. The black box with your ashes is on the dresser in my bedroom. In the summer, we will spread them at the cottage, a place you loved very much. Every morning, before I get out of bed, I look at our wedding picture and say hello. In the evening before I go to sleep, I blow you a kiss, say goodnight, and tell you miss you. I don't think you would mind me chronicling our journey since you always supported me in my every endeavor. You were the wind beneath my wings.

I subscribe to "GriefSteps: 365 Days of Grief" from sympathyplan.com, recommended by the funeral home. Every morning, it sends a helpful email about grieving with quotes from the likes of Elisabeth Kubler-Ross, Ann Lamott, C.S. Lewis, Jodi Picoult, and others. On my laptop, I created a folder for the emails, so I can go back and read them. There have been posts on my Facebook page about grieving. All are helpful. However, there is no "right" way to grieve, just honor it by letting it come when it wants to come.

February 29, 2024

Liberation! I felt like I had been released from prison. After seven long and exceedingly difficult weeks my foot healed completely, I was able to drive again and was supremely happy I didn't have to ask someone to drive me places I needed to go.

However, the podiatrist said to ease slowly into normal activity by alternating wearing the shoe and the boot for two weeks. I return on March 14th and hope I will be able to go back to exercise class and walk Jack.

March 14, 2024

I have been cleared to return to normal activity. There is still pain in my foot and that will take a month or two to go away. Jack returned home. We were so glad to see each other, but because of the pain in my foot, walking him is slow.

Would I have felt your spirit if I were still in our house? Maybe. Do I think grieving slowly throughout the years helped me when you finally left me? Yes. However, your abrupt decline at the end was distressing. I thought you might have made it until summer.

As I take my jacket out of the hall closet, I look at the empty hangers on the right side. I feel empty. There is a hole in my heart that your big loving personality used to occupy. I must be patient and gentle with myself to allow whenever grief comes and to honor your memory by speaking about you as much as possible. The picture of you and me that was on the table at the funeral home is right in front of me as I type. I look at it every day and am grateful for the time we had together. We had a good marriage.

You gave the greatest hugs. I miss you and those hugs immensely. I will hold onto the good memories and try not to dwell on the not-so-good ones. I read this somewhere, but I can't remember where: "The pain of great love is when you have to let go."

When I drive over the bridge, I look down at the roof of your care facility. Sometimes, I wonder what the residents are doing. My daily routine has changed. Caring for you was my purpose. I will need to fill in the void of seeing you every day. I will need a new purpose.

December 19, 2024

This is the first anniversary of your death. It was a hard day reliving the events of last year. Will other anniversaries get easier? I suppose they will. The months flew by as they aways do. It was also a long year for me not only because of grieving but because of my injury and the isolation that occurred. I hope 2025 is a better year.

January 20, 2025

Today is MLK day, the inauguration (ugh), and the one-year anniversary of your Memorial Service. As it was in 2024, we are enduring a polar vortex with dangerously below zero windchills. Jack "told" me he had to go out at 9 AM by staring at me. He is not a barker. I wished he would have waited until later. But I bundled up in layers. I pulled the eyeholes down on the face mask, so I could accommodate my glasses. After I put Jack's coat on, we went out the garage door and were hit with a blast of frigid air. Jack was a trooper. He did his business quickly, and we hurried home.

As I sat down in the chair before my computer, I looked at the picture of you and me and said good morning. I told you your son and his family had to evacuate for one day because a fire erupted near their condo, but I assured you they were fine now although they are not working because their schools are in an evacuation zone.

Today, a picture popped on Facebook. It was a family picture taken after your service. I remember it as a convivial time. People looked at the picture boards, sometimes remarking that they remembered when a particular picture was taken. This was the day to say goodbye to a good man. We all hold your memory in our hearts.

Every person before being diagnosed with Alzheimer's was a different individual. On the next page is a snapshot of the man I married.

Remembering Paul Siket

Paul was born on August 5, 1945, in Shamokin, Pennsylvania, to Andrew and Veronica Siket. He had one older sister and brother and three younger brothers.

Paul was an athlete, playing Little League baseball, and basketball. In high school, he was the starting quarterback for two years and chosen an All-State Quarterback. His brother, Tom, said he was not a braggart. As an Eagle Scout, he would always help with anything whether it was at home or outside. His first job was delivering newspapers with his brother, Tom. For two and a half years, they delivered 80 to 90 newspapers per day, starting at 5 AM.

During the Vietnam War, Paul enlisted in the Navy. He served four years on a transport carrier where he was a supply clerk. He did his job well and received commendations from his superiors. He was honorably discharged early because of migraine headaches.

Paul studied accounting at Penn State University and Muhlenberg College after his release from the Navy.

His son, Eric, was born on April 5, 1976. Paul was always active in his son's life, even after he and his wife divorced. He coached Eric in Little League, and in the summer, they went on long camping trips.

In the summer of 1983, he met his second wife, Christine Calhoun, at a public swimming pool in Allentown,

Pennsylvania. Chris came with a friend, and Paul was there with his son.

For 25 years, Paul worked as an accountant for the Greif Companies in Allentown, Pennsylvania, a manufacturer of men's designer suits. At the end of his time with the company, Paul was the Assistant Controller. In the 1990s, after the Grief Companies closed its doors, he worked as a temporary employee for a few years in Allentown.

While driving to work on a country road, Paul hit black ice, and his Ford Explorer went airborne over the barrier and landed on its wheels in a creek in a gully. The Explorer was totaled. He crawled out of the sunroof, up an embankment, and flagged someone who took him to the hospital. He was lucky to come out of this accident alive, and this had a profound effect on him.

In 1999, after this life-changing event, Paul and his wife moved to her home state of Wisconsin. His son was living in California. His parents were deceased, and it seemed like a suitable time to make a life change.

Paul found a job as the Assistant Controller for Candle Corporation. He worked there until 2010 when the company closed its doors. Although he wanted to continue to work, Paul, as an older worker was never able to find a permanent job. He continued to work temporary jobs as they were available.

Summers were spent at Chris's family cottage. Paul would happily do whatever was asked of him. He and Chris (dog included) enjoyed their rides at dusk around the lake in the fishing boat. He loved sailing and floating around on "his" raft, visiting other piers, and chatting with the people he didn't know.

For several years, Paul was the head usher at his church, a volunteer for AARP in its free tax return preparation service for low-income seniors, treasurer for three non-profits, wrapped gifts at the mall for Habitat for Humanity, poured beer at Octoberfest, gave blood on a regular basis, and during heavy snowstorms cleared snow from an elderly neighbor's driveway. A friend said he is a shining example for all of us.

Paul was an avid Packers fan, kept the garden free of weeds, loved the outdoors, and enjoyed traveling.

REFLECTIONS ON PAUL FROM CHRIS'S SISTER, JACKIE CALHOUN SMITH:

"I met Paul while visiting my sister, Chris, who had moved from Allentown to

Rockaway, New Jersey. She and I drove to Cape May at the southern tip of New Jersey, then crossed the state through the Pine Barrens to New Hope, PA on the Delaware River. We drove north along the river to Bethlehem, where we had lunch with Paul at a restaurant on the river.

At the time, I thought Paul was nervous about meeting me because he talked too much. I realized later that he was just being Paul, friendly, and talkative. I remember Chris saying he was hesitant about her moving in with him because he was worried that it would give the wrong impression to his son, Eric. But Chris left New Jersey and moved into a lovely two-story duplex in Allentown with Paul. Huge trees graced their street. The sycamore out front was one of them. The backyard was a postage stamp with a garage on an alley.

On one of the hottest days of the year, May 23, 1992, they married. Our family converged on their home. Paul's family lived in Pennsylvania and Florida. The air conditioning went out at the reception, and we sweated but had a fun time, as did the new wife and groom.

Until they moved to Appleton, WI after The Grief Company closed, I saw them mostly when they visited the cottage. Paul would bring Eric and one of his friends with them on those vacations. I do not know how old Eric was when Paul and his first wife divorced, but Paul did not get custody. He spent as much time as allowed with Eric. He attended all Eric's school events and went with him to visit colleges when the time came. He was such a good father.

Chris and Paul moved to Appleton in 1999. In 2000, they bought a house not far from ours. That was when I really began to know Paul. He worked hard at finding a permanent job. Age discrimination caught up with him. He took part-time jobs, until the permanent job in Oshkosh. Paul never sat still for long. He was always doing something.

He kept the shed and boathouse in order at the lake. He and I stained all the buildings twice. He and Chris were there to rake in the spring. He cut down dead trees and split the wood for both fireplaces. He cooked on the outside fireplace and was always Chris's sous chef. Wherever and whenever he could help, he would.

Even now Paul is a gentleman, opening doors for women. He always greets company with a smile. In all the years, I've known him, I've only seen him angry once and that was justified but did not last long. He's naturally cheerful, kind, polite and welcoming. He's a sweet man."

A TRIBUTE FROM PAUL'S SON, ERIC:

This is a letter I should have written years ago, but I think I was too afraid to write it. To be honest, my dad and I have a great relationship (well, at least before the disease took hold). However, we were never ones to share "our feelings" or get overly emotional. I only wish I would have gotten over that and been able to share some of this with my dad while he could still comprehend and understand my sentiments. Being a father now myself, I think about my dad every day, and I see him in myself in the way that I father my daughter. It breaks my heart that he didn't get to see me be a father before the disease took hold. I'll always remember one thing my dad told me when my daughter was much younger and before the disease progressed to the stage it is in today; he confided in me that he was proud of the way I was raising India, and he thought I was doing a good job.

Two things I remember most about growing up with my dad is that he loved being a goofball and that he was always present. In fact, most of my cousins would call my dad Uncle Bozo because he was always willing to be goofy and be willing to not take himself too seriously, regardless of who was around. I love more than anything being goofy with my daughter and trying to make her laugh, something I don't even always do with my wife. And every time I do something goofy; I am reminded of my dad and his sense of humor. He really was "the dad joke" personified. My dad's willingness to put himself out there also meant that he was ridiculously friendly. He could start a conversation with almost anyone and be friends with them after 30 minutes. I'll admit, I am not nearly as outgoing as my dad was, but I will still strike up a conversation with other dads at playgrounds. My daughter always asks, "Do you know that person after we leave? I say no, just being friendly. But I know I learned that from watching my dad striking up a conversation with anyone that was willing to chat with him. Unfortunately, now due to the disease my dad rarely likes to talk, even with family members.

My dad was present in just about every aspect of my life, even if at times I didn't want him there – but looking back on it now, I am so thankful for his presence. My parents were divorced when I was young, but my dad never stopped being around. He came to all my baseball games, swimming competitions, cross-country meets and any other extracurricular activity I asked him to come to (from preschool through high school). He even came to stuff I didn't ask him to come to. And this didn't end when I graduated from high school or moved away to California. Even as an adult myself, my dad was present. I began racing trail ultra marathons and triathlons in my 30's and my dad came to 2 competitions to cheer me on, even though I was racing for more than 3 hours. Just being there meant a lot – and I only hope to be able to follow my dad's lead for my own daughter.

My dad introduced me to so many new opportunities. He didn't seem to be afraid to try anything. He was always looking for new adventures to take me on as I was growing up. For many summers, we would have a 2-week father/son camping trip up and down the East Coast, with each summer being a new location. I remember traveling to Niagara Falls in an RV, visiting Colonial Williamsburg, and touring the Baseball Hall of Fame in upstate NY. There are so many places we visited together, and my love of travel and adventure is due in part to him introducing me to all those places. The funniest thing about my dad is he loved to collect brochures. Just about every location we went to, he got a brochure. He even collected brochures from places we didn't visit. I guess back before the internet and smart phones, he was always researching new places for us to see and things to do. He rarely said no to adventures either. He took me skiing and ice skating and sledding for the first time, I learned how to water ski with him, and he would even ride the same roller coaster with me 8 times in a row if I wanted to. I also saw my first world series in person and my first college football game with him. Visiting baseball stadiums is still one of my favorite pastimes in the spring and summer. Unfortunately, now with the disease he rarely likes to venture too far from home and without my stepmom. That was never my dad.

My dad also instilled in me the power of hard work and giving back all which he modeled himself. I remember my dad routinely volunteering at church and he rarely stopped to relax on vacation. He was always cleaning or completing some project or fixing something that needed to be fixed. My daughter now comments how I am always doing something or being "busy" at home. When I joined the cross-country team my freshmen year, my dad even mapped and spray-painted run routes for me on vacation. I dreaded getting up on vacation to run those routes. But fast forward to today, and I have no problem getting up before dawn to run in cold temperatures in the winter or get up before dawn on summer vacation to run 15 miles. I would have told you were crazy if you thought I would be doing that when I grew up, but that groundwork was laid for me at any early age by my dad. When I didn't make the baseball team my freshmen year, my dad worked with me daily throughout the entire summer and winter practicing hitting drills. The spring of my sophomore year, I earned a starting a spot on the high school baseball team. I couldn't have done that without the hours of drills with my dad. It is important to also state how humble my dad was. He never bragged about his abilities or took credit for any work that he assisted me with.

I learned how to play a mean game of checkers and Uno with him on many weekend nights when my parents were first divorced. I also remember some of the "bachelor" meals we had together those first few years – including steak at Ponderosa almost every Friday night and Kraft macaroni and cheese (with canned stewed tomatoes) almost every Saturday night, followed by watching 80's sitcoms. I should note that my dad became a much, much better cook after meeting my stepmom.

My dad wasn't perfect, but I don't really think any dad is perfect and that's ok. I remember specific times when he embarrassed me. One incident occurred while my dad coached Little League. I remembered him showing up to practice wearing some old, ripped sweatpants that just looked terrible. But isn't the job of every father to occasionally embarrass their kid? The important thing he was there, and he was trying!

There are so many more experiences I can write about to try to give you a picture of the man my dad was. I remember going to Bathtub beach with him in Florida at my grandparents' house, routinely racing him in the swimming pool and then one day in middle school being able to beat him. I went canoeing with him down the Delaware river in Cub Scouts, hiking with him and my cousin yearly at Rickets Glenn in PA. We set off illegal fireworks at Lake Winona in PA and built a go-cart from scratch. And the list goes on.

Per the Center for Disease Control's 2024 website:

In 2023, as many as 6.7 million Americans were living with Alzheimer's disease. The number of people living with the disease doubles every five years beyond age 65. This number is projected to nearly triple to 14 million people by 2060.